REMARKABLE CHILDREN

SACAGAWEA

T H E   J O U R N E Y   T O   T H E   W E S T

A Picture-Book Biography

The information for the Remarkable Children Series was

gathered from old letters, journals, and other historical documents.

For Michael Louis Fradin, From Dad, With Love.
D.F.
To my courageous, exploring boys, with love,
N.K.

Consultant:Dr. Merle Wells, Idaho State Historical Society

Text copyright ©1998 by Dennis Fradin
Illustrations copyright © 1998 by Nora Koerber
Photo credits: Photo Research by Susan Van Etten; p. 32, Top, © Peter Lourie; Bottom, © John
Reddy; back cover, Sacajawea © Harry Jackson 1977

Published by Silver Press
A Division of Simon & Schuster
299 Jefferson Road, Parsippany, NJ 07054

Designed by Brooks Design

Printed in the United States of America

ISBN 0-382-39488-7 (LSB) 10 9 8 7 6 5 4 3 2 1
ISBN 0-382-39489-5 (pbk) 10 9 8 7 6 5 4 3 2 1

Library of Congress Cataloging-in-Publication Data
Fradin, Dennis B.
Sacagawea: journey to the west/by Dennis Fradin: illustrated by Nora Koerber.
p. cm. — (Remarkable children series: #4)
Summary: The true story of a Shoshoni Indian girl who served as interpreter, peacemaker, and
guide for the Lewis and Clark Expedition to the Northwest in 1805-1806.
1. Sacagawea, 1786-1884—Juvenile literature. 2. Shoshoni women—Biography—Juvenile literature. 3. Shoshoni Indians—Biography—Juvenile literature. 4. Lewis and Clark Expedition(1804-
1806)—Juvenile literature. [1. Sacagawea, 1786-1884. 2. Shoshoni Indians—Biography. 3. Indians
of North America—Biography. 4. Women—Biography. 5. Lewis and Clark Expedition (1804-1806.]
I. Koerber, Nora, ill. II. Title. III. Series.
F592.7.S123F73   1997   96-16063
978'.004974'0092—dc20   CIP   [B]   AC

REMARKABLE CHILDREN

SACAGAWEA

THE JOURNEY TO THE WEST

The true story of a Shoshoni Indian girl who served as interpreter, peacemaker, and guide for the Lewis and Clark Expedition to the Northwest in 1805-1806.

BY DENNIS FRADIN • ILLUSTRATED BY NORA KOERBER

Silver Press

Parsippany, New Jersey

It has been said that Sacagawea (pronounced Sa ca ga WEE ah or Sa CA ga wee ah) is honored by the most memorials of any American woman. At least four mountain peaks and two lakes are named for her. About twenty-five statues and historical markers also honor her memory. Yet few Americans know who Sacagawea was, and fewer still realize that her great achievements came when she was only about sixteen years old.

The girl who became known as Sacagawea was born around 1789 in what is now Idaho. Little is known of her first years. We don't even know her names, which probably kept changing according to the custom of her people, the Shoshoni Indians. Still, we can reconstruct what her early life may have been like.

Her village probably contained a few dozen people. Her family, which included a brother Cameahwait (CA ME ah wait), lived in a tent called a tepee. While still a baby, she grew accustomed to crossing the mountains and valleys as her people hunted mountain sheep, buffalo, and fished for salmon. They also gathered berries and camas plants, the flowers of which were so blue that fields of them looked like lakes.

Her mother taught the girl how to make bread out of camas and to sew animal skins into clothing. The elders told her stories about how Coyote had created human beings, and warned her about the Nunumbi, "Little People," who shot invisible arrows at those they disliked. With other children, she ran races and learned to juggle mud balls.

The girl's pleasant childhood ended abruptly when she was about eleven. One night in the year 1800, while her people were camped in what is now Montana, her people were attacked by Hidatsa Indians. The girl and her family ran outside their tepee and saw a horrible sight. The raiders were killing adults and seizing children as prisoners.

With the screams of her wounded relatives and friends ringing in her ears, the girl ran toward the river. She was wading across when an enemy warrior rode into the water and pulled her onto his horse. She and several other captured children were forced to travel more than five hundred miles eastward to a Hidatsa village near what is now Bismarck, North Dakota. There the girl was made a slave. She was given the Hidatsa

name Sacagawea which means Bird Woman. It was said that most of the young captives soon escaped but that Sacagawea would not abandoned a crippled friend.

Sacagawea had lived among the Hidatsas for about a year or two when Toussaint Charbonneau visited the village. The big, bearded French trader bought Sacagawea from the Hidatsas and took her to his home in a nearby Mandan Indian village. Charbonneau told Sacagawea she was now his wife, but really she was his slave. She had to cook and do his other housework, and when she didn't obey him fast enough, he beat her.

In 1803, the United States made a deal with France that would change Sacagawea's life. The nation bought a huge piece of land west of the Mississippi River which later became fifteen states. President Thomas Jefferson sent an expedition under Captains Meriwether Lewis and William Clark to learn about this new territory. The explorers set out near St. Louis, Missouri, in May, hoping to travel to the Pacific Ocean. That fall, they came to the North Dakota Indian village where Sacagawea and Charbonneau lived. They built Fort Mandan as their winter quarters.

Charbonneau learned that Lewis and Clark were looking for someone to communicate with the Shoshoni, from whom they hoped to obtain goods for horses later on the trip. He took Sacagawea to the explorers and said that she could do the job because she was a Shoshoni. Charbonneau offered to accompany the expedition with Sacagawea for five hundred dollars. Lewis and Clark were reluctant, for Sacagawea would be the only female among about thirty-five men, plus she was pregnant. Yet she was strong, very eager to go, and could speak Shoshoni. The explorers accepted the offer.

As part of the expedition, Sacagawea and Charbonneau spent the winter in Fort Mandan. There, on February 11, 1805, 16-year-old Sacagawea gave birth to a baby boy. Charbonneau gave their son a French name—Jean Baptiste. But Sacagawea called him Pomp, from a Shoshoni word meaning "Leader."

On the afternoon of April 7, 1805, Sacagawea strapped eight-week-old Pomp to her back and left Fort Mandan with the men. As the eight canoes floated up the Missouri River, she was probably the most eager of

the travelers. She clung to a slender hope that, if any of her people were alive, she would meet them on the journey to the west.

Sacagawea helped the expedition from the start. She saw that the men disliked their dinners of corn-meal and dry meat, and began gathering plants near the riverbanks. The strawberries, plums, and other edible plant foods she found were tastier and healthi-er than the expedition's usual meals.

Captain Lewis often walked along the shore with his huge Newfoundland dog, Scammon, but Captain Clark frequently joined Sacagawea as she searched for edible plants. The red-haired Clark grew very fond of Sacagawea, whom he nicknamed Janey. Once when Charbonneau hit her, Clark warned him never to do that again. Sacagawea's baby playing by the campfire, also delighted Clark. At night before they went to sleep in the big leather tent, Clark held Pomp on his knees and sang to him.

Much of the time, Sacagawea and Charbonneau traveled with the two captains in a white pirogue, a 50-foot canoe with a sail. On the foggy afternoon of

May 14, 1805, Charbonneau was steering the vessel as Lewis and Clark walked along the shore. Suddenly, a wind gust tipped the pirogue which filled with water. The two captains watched helplessly from 1,000 feet away as their supplies, which included trade goods and medicines, began to float away. Without these items, the expedition might have to turn back.

Charbonneau, who was about forty-five years old, began crying that he could not swim. Sacagawea knew she could swim to shore with Pomp on her back if the pirogue sank. She calmly plucked the floating items out of the water as several men bailed out the vessel with cooking kettles. Within a few minutes, the pirogue was righted and Sacagawea had saved many of the supplies. Both captains praised Sacagawea for her "fortitude and resolution" during the crisis.

The travelers had many other problems. There were clashes with grizzly bears, dangerous rapids, and mosquitoes so thick they made Scammon howl at night. Once Sacagawea and Clark barely escaped being bitten by rattlesnakes. Another time, Sacagawea became so ill it was feared she would die. A few days

after she recovered, she and Pomp explored a ravine with Charbonneau and Clark. Sacagawea had just placed Pomp on a rock ledge, perhaps to change his cattail cotton diaper, when a storm hit. She scooped up Pomp and climbed to safety with the two men, seconds before the ravine filled with water.

In July the expedition reached Sacagawea's home country. She helped guide the men through familiar lands, even showing them where she had been captured five years earlier. As they neared what is now Idaho, the captains grew desperate to find the Shoshoni. Winter was approaching, and they needed horses to carry their supplies through the mountains. Lewis scouted ahead with three other men, and on August 13 they reached a Shoshoni camp. Using sign language, Lewis convinced the chief to come meet the rest of the expedition. But dozens of warriors who accompanied the chief suspected that Lewis was leading them into a trap.

When a large number of white men with guns came into view, Lewis feared that the panicky Shoshoni Indians might attack. This was a crossroads

in American history, for England might try to seize the Northwest if the Lewis and Clark Expedition failed. The warriors were reaching for their bows when they saw something that eased their fears.

An Indian girl with a baby on her back was with the white men. When she realized who the Indians were, Sacagawea danced about and said in sign language, "These are my people!" By an incredible stroke of luck, they had found her band of Shoshoni, now led by her brother Chief Cameahwait. Sacagawea ran to Cameahwait and threw her blanket over him as a sign of love. But after the Indians and explorers entered the tent, Sacagawea burst into tears when she learned that most of their relatives had died in the Hidatsa raid. Her only living relatives, besides Cameahwait, were a brother who was away and their sister's son.

Still, Sacagawea had a job to do. She and several others translated her brother's words from Shoshoni to Hidatsa to French to English in a kind of relay. In return for clothing and other goods, Cameahwait agreed to provide the expedition with horses and a guide to lead them over the mountains.

As the explorers and Indians celebrated with food and songs, Sacagawea must have been tempted to leave the expedition and rejoin her people. She couldn't, though, for Charbonneau might demand to keep Pomp. When the expedition moved on, Sacagawea said good-bye to Cameahwait and her old friends, knowing that she probably would never see any of them again.

The mountain crossing was extremely difficult. Snow fell and was soon knee deep. Food was so scarce that the travelers had to kill and eat some of their horses. Walking through the cold and the snow was an ordeal for the men. It was much harder for Sacagawea, who also had to carry and protect Pomp.

Several more times on the westward journey the expedition met Indians. The Native Americans might have attacked an all-male group. When they saw Sacagawea and Pomp, they befriended and fed the travelers. As Clark noted in his journal: "A woman with a party of men is a token of peace."

Rain became a problem as they approached the Pacific Ocean. At one point it rained every day for about two weeks. Along the Columbia River, the

travelers had to dodge 100-foot trees that tore loose from the muddy riverbanks and crashed into the water. Finally, in November of 1805, the exhausted explorers reached their goal. Near present-day Astoria, Oregon, they built Fort Clatsop for their winter quarters. Sacagawea and her baby had traveled about 2,500 miles from Fort Mandan to the Pacific Coast.

That winter, when a Chinook Indian visited them, Lewis and Clark admired his sea otter robe. They thought it would make fine gift for President Jefferson but, the Indian would only trade it for Sacagawea's blue bead waist belt. She handed over her belt, receiving in exchange from Lewis and Clark a blue cloth coat.

Sacagawea was not so meek when a whale washed onto the nearby shore. Upon learning that some of the men planned to go see the giant creature without her, she grew angry. Lewis and Clark recorded that she said: "I have traveled a long way with you. It is very hard not to be permitted to see the great waters, [the ocean] and now also the monstrous fish." She got her wish and took Pomp in his cradle-board to see the whale.

Pomp celebrated his first birthday on February 11, 1806. By then he must have been learning to say a few words and walk, for Clark soon was referring to him as "my little dancing boy." Six weeks later, in late March, the expedition left Fort Clatsop and began the long journey home.

Illness and hunger again plagued the travelers on the return trip. Sacagawea again proved invaluable, even helping choose the best routes. A grateful Clark praise her "great service to me as a pilot through this country." He showed his love for Pomp, whom he called Pompey, by naming a 200-foot-tall rock in southeast Montana "Pompey's Pillar."

The travelers reached Fort Mandan in August after a five-month journey. Clark paid Charbonneau his five hundred dollars. Then Sacagawea, Pomp, and Charbonneau left the Lewis and Clark Expedition, which continued on to St. Louis.

Sacagawea had aided in a major exploration and helped the Untied States take control of the Northwest. Yet, as Charbonneau's slave, she received no reward. Captain William Clark, missed Pomp so much that he

soon wrote to Charbonneau, begging to adopt the boy. Perhaps because Sacagawea would not part with Pomp, Clark did not get to adopt Pomp just then.

Tall tales have been told about Sacagawea's later life. One is that she died on a Wyoming Indian reservation at nearly one hundred years of age. Sadly, the real Sacagawea seems to have died of a fever at a Missouri River trading post on December 20, 1812, at the age of only about 23. She left behind an infant daughter, Lizette, who may not have lived very long, and seven-year-old Pomp. Clark adopted Pomp and sent him to school in St. Louis. Pomp became one of the best-educated people of his time, even serving as an *alcalde* (similar to a mayor) of a Spanish community in California.

As for Sacagawea, her fame has grown with the passage of time. Today the teenaged girl who accompanied Lewis and Clark is remembered as one of the great heroines in United States' history.

REMINDERS OF SACAGAWEA

Besides monuments, many landmarks have been named for Sacagawea, whose name is also spelled Sacajawea or Sakakawea. These landmarks include North Dakota's Lake Sakakawea, Oregon's Sacajawea Peak, and Washington's Sacajawea State Park.

Lake Sakakawea, North Dakota

Monument of Sacagawea with Lewis and Clark at Fort Benton, Montana

Sacajewea Peak, Montana